W
Best Lost
Treasure
Stories

C. B. Colby

 Sterling Publishing Co., Inc.   New York

Library of Congress Cataloging-in-Publication Data

Colby, C. B. (Carroll B.)
    World's best lost treasure stories / C.B. Colby ; new
illustrations for this edition by Elise Chanowitz.
        p.   cm.
    Includes index.
    Summary: Thirty-six brief accounts of lost treasures and the
circumstances of their disappearance.
    ISBN 0-8069-8420-1
    1. Treasure-trove—Juvenile literature.   [1. Buried treasure.]
I. Chanowitz, Elise, ill.   II. Title.
G525.C645   1991
904—dc20   91-14377
                                                            CIP
                                                            AC

10   9   8   7   6   5   4   3   2   1

First paperback edition published in 1992 by
Sterling Publishing Company, Inc.
387 Park Avenue South, New York, N.Y. 10016
© 1991 by C.B. Colby
New illustrations © 1991 by Elise Chanowitz
This edition compiled and adapted from
Strangely Enough! and *The Weirdest People in the World* by C.B. Colby
Distributed in Canada by Sterling Publishing
℅ Canadian Manda Group, P.O. Box 920, Station U
Toronto, Ontario, Canada M8Z 5P9
Distributed in Great Britain and Europe by Cassell PLC
Villiers House, 41/47 Strand, London WC2N 5JE, England
Distributed in Australia by Capricorn Link Ltd.
P.O. Box 665, Lane Cove, NSW 2066
Manufactured in the United States of America
All rights reserved

Sterling ISBN 0-8069-8420-1 Trade
                0-8069-8421-X Paper

CONTENTS

Note from the Author

Treasure can be of many kinds and located almost anywhere. You can rarely count on finding it. But once you do find it, and even after you spend it, there remains a lifetime of intriguing conjecture on the strange people and circumstances that put it within your reach.

Many of the stories in this book came from total strangers I met casually while tracking down others of the list. Some were sent to me anonymously by readers of my column. Others came from long-forgotten diaries, family and town histories. Some were told to me by friends and neighbors.

Are they all true? The people who reported them believed that they were. But whether they all are—or not—I hope you have as much fun reading them as I had tracking them down.

1. FABULOUS TREASURE

- Unpacked from the backs of 11,000 llamas, one of the world's really great missing treasures lies hidden in the mountains of Peru.

- A sacred lake in Colombia may be one of the richest treasure-troves in the world.

- Nineteen men were murdered for the gold that now lies in a sand-covered charcoal heap near San Antonio.

- The Lost Padre Mine—we know where it is, but can't find the way in.

Lost Inca Treasure

The Aztecs and Incas who lived in Mexico and South America were known for their fabulous treasures of gold. The gold was so plentiful that they not only adorned their temples and shrines with it, but made all their household articles from this costly metal.

When Pizarro invaded the Inca territory, he captured the emperor Atahualpa and held him for ransom. In payment for their leader's release, the Incas led 11,000 treasure-laden llamas through the mountains of Peru. Deep in the mountains, while en route to the appointed spot, the bearers received word by runner that Pizarro had treacherously murdered Emperor Atahualpa in spite of the fact that the vast ransom was on its way. The angry and sorrowful Incas felt there was no need to continue the trip any longer.

Realizing that Pizarro would still seek out the treasure, they unloaded it from the backs of the shaggy beasts and hid it away in the many caves and valleys of the mountains. The gold was concealed so cleverly, and the secret of its hiding place was so well kept, that to this day the enormous fortune is still one of the few really great missing treasures of the world.

A few pieces have turned up—a statue studded with jewels and three solid gold coffins—but they only help keep alive the story of the vast missing hoard of treasure. Somewhere, deep in the mountains of Peru, lies an enormous hoard, waiting for some lucky searcher to find it.

Lake of Gold

If you were told where someone had thrown a vast treasure, you'd think it would be a simple matter to rush right over and pick it up, wouldn't you? Well, it's not always that easy, even when you know just where it is. This is the situation in Lake Guatavita, high in the Cordillera Mountains of Colombia, one of the greatest treasure-trove areas in the world.

This lake, 10,000 feet up in the mountains north of Santa Fe de Bogotá, was for centuries the scene of wild ceremonies when chiefs were crowned or religious observances took place. As part of the ritual, when a new Inca chief was installed, he gilded himself with a coating of pure gold dust and plunged under the sacred waters of the lake.

In connection with these ceremonies, the natives threw vast quantities of gold, jewels and other valuables into the waters from the shore. At other times, to appease various gods whole villages gathered their valuables, marched to the lake shore and threw the treasures into the water. Once, to foil a Spanish invader, the chief of the Chibcha tribe threw more than two tons of gold into the lake. Altogether, it is estimated that almost six billion dollars' worth of treasure is at the bottom of Lake Guatavita.

Yet all the many attempts to locate this vast hoard have failed to turn up more than a few small gold images, jewels and coins.

Why? In the first place, the lake is a thousand feet wide at its narrowest point, and reaches a depth of more than a thousand feet. At its shallowest part, it is still nearly fifty feet deep, and no one knows exactly where the treasure was thrown from the shore. Over the ages, sediment, rotten vegetation and mud have settled in layer upon layer over the vast treasure below the surface.

One English salvage company did attempt to retrieve a part of the great fortune from the bottom, but it only recovered a few hundred dollars' worth—hardly enough to pay them back for the great expense of the expedition. It seems that it would take a vast amount of machinery, diving equipment and money to even begin an effective salvage operation.

Maximilian's Millions

Somewhere in Texas, near Castle Gap, about fifteen miles east of the Horse Head Crossing of the Pecos River, lies a treasure estimated to be worth between four and five million dollars. The following story is one of the many tragic incidents connected with this vast hoard of lost treasure.

While the United States was in the midst of the Civil War, Napoleon III of France put Archduke Maximilian of Austria on the Mexican throne against the wishes of the Mexican people. The new emperor brought with him his personal fortune, and during his stay in Mexico, added still more gold and jewels to it. However, he was afraid that he would never live to enjoy his riches, and rightly so.

In 1866, a year before he was dethroned and executed, he decided to send his fortune to San Antonio, Texas, for safekeeping. It never got there, and it has never been found.

The treasure, loaded into fifteen oxcarts, was guarded by four Austrian friends of the emperor. The fifteen drivers were told that the carts were full of barrels of flour and they set out for the border and safety. Once across the border, they met six ex-Confederate soldiers who told them the route to San Antonio was beset with hostile Indians and highwaymen. The Austrians hired the ex-soldiers to go with them as guards.

One night the soldiers discovered that the "flour" was treasure and decided that they would get it for them-

selves. The next night, near Castle Gap, they murdered
the Austrians and the Mexican drivers. Then they
buried the bulk of the treasure with the bodies over it,
and burned the carts. Charred embers were the only
visible remains when the six murderers set out for San
Antonio to spend the money they took with them and to
get help to bring in the rest of the huge fortune.

On the way, one of the men became sick and stopped
to rest, urging the others to go ahead without him. They
believed that he was faking and planning to get more of
the treasure for himself. So they shot him and left him
for dead.

But the wounded man was not dead, and in a day or so
he was able to hobble on after his would-be murderers.
Shortly thereafter, he came upon their bodies. They had
been murdered and robbed.

He kept on and stopped at a camp of horse thieves for
the night.

That very night the thieves were captured by a sher-
iff's posse and the wounded man was thrown into jail
with the others. Later he was set free, but a doctor told
him that he would soon die of blood poisoning. In his last
moments he drew a crude map showing where the treasure was buried, and gave it to the doctor.

After the renegades and Indians had been driven from
the area, the doctor tried to follow the map to the spot
where the carts were burned. He was unable to find it.
Somewhere under a sand-covered charcoal heap lies the
vast treasure, guarded by the bones of nineteen men
who never reached their goal.

The Lost Padre Mine

Somewhere in the side of Franklin Mountain, near El Paso, Texas, is one of the richest and most famous of lost treasures—the fabulous Lost Padre Mine, in which is said to be buried not only vast secret hoards but a good deal of gold ore.

The Lost Padre Mine was worked for many years in the early 1700s before it finally began to peter out. It was not forgotten, however. In 1780, some Jesuit priests, expelled from Mexico, reportedly dumped three hundred jack loads (mule loads) of silver bullion at the bottom of the entrance shaft, covered it up, and fled, never to return.

Later, Juan de Onate, the founder of New Mexico, added to this rich store. It is said that his contribution to the shaft included treasure that originally came from the vaults of the Aztecs—"4,336 ingots of gold, 5,000 bars of silver and nine mule loads of church ornaments and jewels."

By the time information about this double deposit in the old Padre Mine leaked out, many years had passed. The treasures were sought by many but were never located. There turned out to be more than one shaft to the mine. Many of them were small, hardly large enough for a man to enter. And, hunt as the seekers would, they could not find the right one. Some think that the tunnel shaft was intentionally blasted to cover the secret. Others think that perhaps a natural slide concealed the entrance, or that the last man to visit the shaft—Onate himself—may have started a slide to cover up the treasure. It is known that many shafts, including the main one, collapsed over the years.

It may be that another slide someday will roar down from above and sweep away the rocks from the very shaft that leads to riches probably worth several millions of dollars.

Apparently, no large company or organization today considers an expedition into Franklin Mountain to be worthwhile. Yet hope persists. Annually, several hundred entrepreneurs—young and old—can be found rummaging around the mountain base with shovels and old shoeboxes to hold the loot.

2. HATE— GREED— MURDER @ MADNESS

- He hid his fortune from his wife—under the outhouse!

- A family's greed seals up a cave of Spanish treasure.

- A stone with two crosses on it tells a double-crossing tale.

- Did the gold from the Lost Lemon Mine of Alberta drive Mr. Lemon insane?

No Gold for Elsie

In 1860, a couple named Felix and Elsie Conway lived in the 1200 block on State Street in Chicago, Illinois. They had had a fight, and stopped speaking to each other. They wrote notes if they had to communicate and their marriage lapsed into a silence that lasted 40 years!

Felix became successful in the cattle business, amassing a fortune that he decidedly did not want his wife to inherit. When, at 63, he was informed that he was dying of cancer, he withdrew his money from the bank—cash and securities—and began walking around his property, looking for a place to bury it.

His outhouse was about ready for its periodic move to a new site. Why not include the treasure with the new location? "Perfect!" Felix thought. So he converted $250,000 into gold coins which he smuggled home a few at a time, to avoid detection.

The new outhouse pit was dug six feet wide but eight feet deep rather than the customary five. Felix spread the coins over the bottom of the hole one moonlit night and then poured cement over them to form a solid slab. He filled it in with fresh dirt and later the outhouse was set on this foundation. But his plans for permanent security went awry.

A few months later Felix took a turn for the worse and was advised that death was days away. In panic he told his doctor where he had buried the gold and offered it to him—anything was all right as long as Elsie didn't get her hands on it! The doctor was delighted. All he had to do was wait for Elsie's death to dig up the treasure.

Felix died. Elsie's search for his fortune proved fruitless. The doctor settled down to wait. But fate was against him too, for 18 years later he was dying and the widow was still in excellent health. The doctor now confided in his son, directing that he in turn wait for the widow's death so that he could buy the property and the treasure. The doctor died. The son settled down to wait his chance. But that, too, was not to be.

Widow Conway finally died at 92, a few years after the doctor's son.

Years later, the house on State Street was torn down but no gold hoard was ever reported. Perhaps even now under the foundation of a big building or embedded in a cast-off slab of concrete, the quarter-million in gold still rests.

The Sealed Cave

Every so often an old Indian who lived far back in the New Mexico mountains with his wife and son came into town with a small bar of gold. The bar was always marked with Spanish symbols. Since it was illegal for an individual to possess such gold bars, they were confiscated each time. However, the Indian kept coming back. After a while he revealed that the bars came from a cave in the mountains, but he refused to tell exactly where it was. In addition to the gold, he said, he could see through a small opening that there was far more treasure in the cave, as well as swords, armor and other relics of what might have been a Spanish expedition of long ago. All attempts to spy upon him were foiled.

It wasn't long after the Indian told this story that his trips to town stopped. Nobody saw him for many months. Then, one day, he returned, but he didn't have a bar of gold with him. Asked what happened, he related how his wife and son were eager to get all the treasure. They had urged him to blast open the cave to make access easy, but he refused. So they decided to do it themselves, as soon as they had the chance.

His son obtained some explosives and hid them until the Indian was going to be away. He and his mother figured they could enlarge the opening to the inner cave, which had closed up over the years by the shifting of the rocks in the cavern.

As soon as the Indian left, his wife and son set about their project with enthusiasm. But they had too much enthusiasm—and too much powder—for when the explosive charge went off, it worked in reverse.

The explosion brought down most of the interior of the cavern, sealing not only the treasure-filled inner room, but the outer cave, too, where the gold bars were hidden. The entire cavern was buried under tons and tons of rock and earth, forever sealing the treasure within the mountain.

The Stone in Skeleton Canyon

Somewhere in the Peloncillo Mountains in eastern Arizona there is a rugged canyon. One side is a steep cliff while the other is wooded rolling hills. A river runs through the canyon, and somewhere on one of its banks is a squarish stone marked with two crosses, one above the other. Under that stone is a reported treasure of over $3,000,000.

How it got there is a tale of plunderers, double-crossings and murder—part legend, part authentic, and all strange.

Back about 1882, a bunch of smugglers started north from Mexico with a vast treasure carried on pack mules. Word of its approach leaked out in Arizona, and a bandit by the name of Curly Bill Brocius decided to capture it. He sent a pal, Jim Hughes, to find out if the reports were true.

Hughes came back with the news that the caravan would pass through Skeleton Canyon the following August, only to find that Curly Bill was off on another trip and no one knew when he would return. This suited Hughes fine, for he had about decided to take the treasure for himself.

Hughes rounded up Hunt Zwing, a young desperado named Billy Grounds, and a half-dozen other cronies and told them his plans. They agreed not to tell Curly Bill about the coming caravan and began their hijacking preparations. The plan went off well. One night in August the treasure caravan of thirty mules entered the dark Skeleton Canyon pass. The twenty smugglers guarding it did not know that they were being watched. The next morning they stopped to rest near the canyon's mouth and posted guards.

Suddenly shots rang out; three smugglers fell dead, and a stampede started. Mules fled in all directions, spilling gold on the canyon floor. Smugglers ran, fired, and fell until all were killed. The treasure was now in the hands of Hughes and his gang.

It was buried in a huge hole, and the gang returned to Galeyville to let the excitement die down. Hughes then took Zwing and Grounds aside and told them to move the treasure to a different hole so they could divide it without sharing with the others. Zwing and Grounds hired an old Mexican man to help them while Hughes stayed in town. Later he found that they had double-crossed him, killed the Mexican helper and hidden the gold in a spot known only to them.

Later Zwing and Grounds had an argument. Grounds was killed and Zwing wounded. Hughes hurried to

Zwing to find out where the treasure was hidden, but arrived too late. Zwing had already fled, bleeding. But Zwing was dying. He finally revealed the treasure's location to a half-brother, Hugh Zwing, muttering something about a square stone with two crosses on the bank of a creek near a spring. Brother Hugh searched for but never found the bullion. It is reportedly still there—in diamonds, life-size gold church statues, coins, and bars of gold and silver.

The stone in Skeleton Canyon, if it exists, is thus—appropriately enough—marked with a double cross.

The Lost Lemon Mine

The yarn of the Lost Lemon Mine of Alberta Province, Canada, has been told in legend and folk song for many years.

It seems that two men, now known only as Lemon and Blackjack, started off into the vast Alberta wilderness and mountains looking for gold. Unlike most such adventurers, they actually found a mine and made a very rich strike. As a matter of fact, the strike was so enormous that it drove Lemon insane.

After a few days of working the vein and thinking about the fortune literally at his fingertips, Lemon decided to do away with his partner and have it all to himself. He carefully waited his chance and then suddenly fell upon Blackjack one day and killed him in cold blood. Afterwards, he became obsessed with the idea that somebody would find out about his crime, or even already knew about it.

He hastily buried Blackjack's body and left the scene in panic, forgetting about the mine and all its gold. He wanted to flee from his crime before it could be discovered. But he was too late.

Unknown to Lemon, two Indian braves had been watching from a distance when he killed Blackjack. After he had buried the body, they had hastened to their chief with the story not only of the murder but also of the rich mine.

The chief thought it over and decided that if news of

the gold mine leaked out—as it was bound to do if the Indians worked it—a gold rush would ruin their hunting lands and eventually spoil the whole area where the tribe had lived for so many years in peace and prosperity.

His decision was that the two braves were to keep their story secret on pain of death. They were to go to the mine in secret and cover up all its traces so that it could not be found. This they did, so well that years later when the old chief had died and news of the mine's existence leaked out, it could not be found again, even by the two braves.

Oddly enough, everyone who went to Alberta to try to find the mine met with tragic accidents and, in some cases, violent death under unusual circumstances.

3. PIRATES & BANDITS

- What is a pirate ship really like, after it sinks?

- Somewhere near St. Augustine, Florida, is a small fortune in pirate gold.

- Lost—found—lost—found—and lost again— pirate Jean Lafitte's treasure is guarded by the winds.

- Could some of Captain Kidd's treasure be buried in Westchester, New York?

- A strange bargain is struck between an Indian chief and Spanish adventurers.

- Once you have found a hidden treasure— never leave it to come back later. Many have, to their dismay.

Sunken Ships

The bottom of the sea holds its share of buried treasure. The popular version of a sunken pirate ship is a sailing vessel listing a bit to one side, tattered sails moving with the underwater currents, and perhaps a skeleton or two slouching on its decks. We picture the rigging as still pretty much intact and although there are a few holes, the ship might be raised and after a bit of repair sent on its way.

In reality, sunken pirate ships are not at all like this. In the first place, all wooden parts would have been eaten away long ago by Teredo shipworms. The rigging would have rotted and the metal fittings would have broken and sunk to the bottom. Any skeletons would have vanished. Only the heavier metal parts would remain, and the ballast stones would be well covered and concealed with layer upon layer of coral and sand. The sunken ship would look like a low, lumpy, uneven spot in the ocean floor, with perhaps a coral-encrusted cannon or two to give away its location. Finding such a wreck is a lot harder than you'd think, and a job for experienced divers.

About the only sign of such a wreck is the fact that it looks a bit different from the rest of the ocean debris. It helps if you can recognize a cannon under all those layers of coral "cement." Even metal parts are usually reduced to iron oxide, silver oxide or copper oxide. Sea water acts as an electrolyte, and when two metals of a different molecular weight are close together a galvanic current is set up to destroy one of the metals while the other is saved. If, for example, a silver coin rests against an iron nail, the nail will suffer, but the silver will remain pretty much the same. So will pottery and porcelain. Frequently silver or other metals inside an iron chest will stay intact while the chest itself is ruined.

Finding buried treasure, then, is often a matter of knowing what to look for. For example, a shapeless chunk of coral may be taken from the site of a wreck. An X-ray, however, may reveal that it is really a collection of old coins, bar metal, spikes and perhaps even a pewter mug. Recovering such items is a delicate and complicated job for experts, who use chemicals to remove the covering and then fine tools to expose and clean the "hidden" treasure within.

Gasparilla's Legacy

Somewhere down in Florida, near St. Augustine, there is a chest buried by an ancient live oak. In it is a small fortune in pirate gold.

In 1785, Gasparilla, the famed pirate, tired of the risks and hardships of his way of life, decided to become a law-abiding citizen. He planned to leave his pirate headquarters on Gasparilla Island and head for Anastasia Island, just off the coast of St. Augustine, which was then in the hands of the Spaniards.

From there he intended to contact the Spanish governor of St. Augustine, buy the governor's forgiveness, and arrange for sanctuary in that city. That was the only way he could escape from his many enemies. But to carry out his plan, it was necessary to get some cash away from his pirate cronies and hide it where he could lay his hands on it later. This is all recorded in his diary.

He dropped anchor just off Anastasia and, alone, rowed ashore in a small boat. With him was a small chest containing the equivalent of $50,000 in coins. From the ship his henchmen watched him draw the boat onto the beach and stride off into the dense foliage. An hour or so later he returned without the chest and rowed back to the ship.

According to an old document, he went "a short distance inland, turning from the sea marshes into a jungle of palms, sage trees and live oaks, where I travelled about a half an hour, stopping under a large live oak tree where I buried the small chest."

That is the only record of Gasparilla's treasure. The chest of gold may still be there, for the pirate never used it to buy his pardon. A short time after he buried the coins, his ship was seized in Charlotte Harbor, and he jumped overboard to his death. He never returned for the chest and none of his crew knew exactly where the live oak tree was.

By now that tree is probably gone and there may even be a McDonald's or a beach house where it stood. It's too bad that Gasparilla couldn't have been a bit more specific with his directions!

Lafitte's Odd "Bricks"

Jean Lafitte, the famous pirate, spent many years in and around Texas. His ships cruised the Gulf of Mexico, and his treasure was buried not only on the Texas coast itself but on many offshore islands and shoals. There is a tale of one Lafitte treasure that was reportedly found, lost, and found again—only to be lost once more!

Lavaca County, Texas, is located about halfway between San Antonio and Houston and about 50 miles inland from the coast. Through the center of it runs the Lavaca River, which eventually empties into a coastal bay. Lafitte was chased up this river more than once by gunboats, escaping only when the river became too shallow for the larger vessels to follow. Somewhere along this river, this incident took place.

A Lavaca County farmer (some say he was a rancher) took a ride one day across his land and stopped to rest his horse. He dismounted and strolled around the area to stretch his legs. As he came back to his horse, he suddenly noticed what appeared to be a small pile of black bricks half-buried under windblown dirt and brush. Out of idle curiosity he kicked away the dead branches and exposed the ends of several of these odd bricks. He picked two up and was astonished to find how heavy they were.

They did not feel like black clay-baked bricks, nor did they feel like stone. They felt smooth and almost greasy. The farmer stuck one in his saddlebag and galloped off home. On the way, the wind began to pick up, and by the time he reached his buildings a small sandstorm was whirling across the plain behind him. He thought how lucky he was to have started home when he did.

After taking care of his horse, he carried his brick into the house and cleaned it off. He took out his knife and began to scrape at the black surface. Underneath shone the bright gleam of pure silver! What he had brought home was a brick, or bar, of pure silver, quite probably from a cache of treasure left there by Lafitte on one of his escape cruises up the Lavaca River. The farmer could hardly wait for the wind to stop blowing so that he could saddle up again and return to where he had found the little pile of "black bricks" under the sand.

When the storm had died down, he raced back to the area, only to find that the high winds and drifting dirt had concealed all traces of the hidden pile of silver. He never found the treasure again. There are rumors that others had also seen it but hadn't bothered to dismount and investigate. Perhaps it is still there—waiting for a high wind to reveal its hiding place once again.

No Kidd-ing!

Would-be treasure hunters often bemoan the fact that the pirate loot they long for seems to be located somewhere else. It's found in the tropics, the far West, or in other far-off places they have little chance of investigating. There are, however, several spots right around New York City where such treasure is said to lie buried.

For example, some city commuter may now be living over a long-buried pirate hoard along Westchester County's shores. According to a legend popular around Rye Beach, many years ago a stranger begged a night's lodging from a farmer's wife. It was raining and thundering, so in spite of the strange garb of the man, the lady took him in out of the storm, gave him shelter and fed him a good breakfast the next day. To her astonishment the lady was requested to hold out her apron. In payment for her kindness, the oddly dressed stranger opened his pack and filled her apron with gold pieces.

Since that time folks have hunted around Rye Beach for more of what was quickly assumed to be Captain Kidd's treasure. The gold pieces filling the lady's apron, it was said, were pirate gold.

*   *   *

At Croton Point on the Hudson River, 50 miles north of New York City, there is a high hill known on old maps as Money Hill because of a legend that Captain Kidd (and other pirates) buried treasure there. It is reported that old coins, including pieces of eight, have been found on this hill. Kidd's buried hoards have also been reported hidden away at Grassy Point on the Hudson and also around Peekskill, both a few miles to the north of Croton.

*   *   *

At the base of Dunderberg Mountain, just south of the Bear Mountain Bridge, and below the U.S. Military Academy at West Point, legend maintains there is more Kidd treasure buried on what is called Kidd's Point. Further north, on the face of Crow's Nest Mountain, another of his strong boxes is reported to be hidden.

*   *   *

At Sleepy Hollow, near Tarrytown, New York, a skeleton was found many years ago. A local legend quickly grew that Kidd had secreted treasure in the area and had killed a slave who had assisted him in its burial. The legend, of course, may be fact.

*   *   *

It is reported that off Hudson Highlands, near West Point, Kidd's ship, the *Quedah Merchant*, was scuttled after the pirate captured the sloop *San Antonio* and decided to use her instead. A huge hoard of treasure was said to have been removed from the *Quedah Merchant* before it was sunk and subsequently buried along the shores of the Highlands. Is it still there? Could some of the treasure still be on board the sunken ship?

The Deal

Once the shores of Florida were practically littered with Spanish galleon wrecks, and the beaches were strewn with treasures washed up after every storm. The local Indians were not interested, however, and ignored them, except for a few trinkets that they picked up to wear. There was one exception—a chief of the Calusa tribe on Florida's western coast.

This chief's village lay along the shores of Charlotte Harbor, an area that still produces pirate legends. A wise, studious man, he had learned the bartering value of gold and silver with white visitors, so he gathered gold and silver bars from the harbor's wreckage and buried them. News that he had done so soon leaked abroad, and Spaniards arrived to demand the hoard.

The chief refused to tell where the treasure was hidden, except on one condition. The Spaniards were to educate his daughter as a Christian so that she could return to her people and convert them.

The Spaniards were not happy with this proposition. It would take time, possibly years, to indoctrinate the young Indian girl and meanwhile they would have to do without the money. Nevertheless, they agreed. The girl was taken to Havana and entered in a convent.

Unfortunately, the chief's plan backfired. His daughter, once educated in the ways of the white man, apparently preferred them to the rough-and-ready customs of the Calusa Indians. She had no interest in converting them. She fell in love with a wealthy Spanish society leader in Havana. They were soon married and sailed for Madrid to live, leaving the chief with no daughter and the Spaniards with no treasure.

The Spaniards demanded the treasure anyway, claiming they'd fulfilled their part of the bargain by arranging for the girl's education. The chief argued that they had not returned his daughter as he had requested, to Christianize the tribe. He accused the Spaniards of tampering with the girl's mind in some irreligious way, and he refused to tell where the treasure was buried.

To this day that vast pile of gold and silver bars lies beneath some spot along the islands or coast of Charlotte Harbor. Perhaps tomorrow a sunbather will jab his beach umbrella into something hard under the sand and move to a better spot a few feet away, annoyed by the impact between his sunshade and the fortune he never found.

Pot of Gold

Monterrey, Mexico, has been the scene of much lawlessness over the years. It was there that an interesting story began one day in 1885, when five bandits held up and robbed a bank. They escaped with about $18,000. Pursued by the "Rurales," the local law officers, the bandits fled north into Texas. During the chase four of the bandits were killed, but one escaped with the loot, all in gold coins.

When he neared old Fort Belknap, he feared that he would be stopped by the soldiers stationed there. So he hid out for a few days until he saw his chance to steal a cast-iron bean pot from a farmer's house. He put the gold coins into this pot and buried it, expecting to come back for it later when the excitement died down.

Not long after, he met a group of renegades. In the course of an argument, they shot him and rode off, leaving him for dead. Two Texans heard the shots, came to investigate and found him bleeding to death and nearly unconscious. But before he died, he told them about the buried loot and said they could have it in payment for helping him. With his last breath he gave directions: "One mile from Fort Belknap, 256 steps north of a creek, and 86 steps west of a prickly pear tree, it is buried and marked with a swallow fork (stick) and it is buried the depth of a wagon rod with one half the ring showing above ground and three rocks piled against the ring."

The two Texans were pretty skeptical of the bandit's story, but some time later one of them, a man named Carter, decided to see if he could find the location described by the dying man. He retraced the steps of the bandit and finally spotted three stones that seemed to be piled over something. As he began to kick away the stones, he heard a rider coming. It was the owner of the property. Rather than share the treasure with him, Carter said nothing about why he was there and was ordered to leave at once.

Several times later he returned to recover the treasure, but as time passed, dust had covered the half-ring of the wagon rod, the stones all looked alike and the forked stick could not be found. Had nature cheated him out of a fortune or had the owner discovered the ring and then the treasure? Carter never dared to ask questions for fear that he would tip his hand, but unless the owner found and recovered the "pot of gold," it's still there waiting for some lucky person's rainbow to point the way.

4. WAR TO WAR

- Buried in the barrels of iron cannons, the famous Hessian treasure is hidden near Dalton, Massachusetts.

- Hundreds of ships have gone down with valuable cargoes in the Great Lakes—one with a British army payroll.

- Millions in gold are buried under the "Little Versailles of Louisiana."

- Burying treasure in the ground seems like the safest way to hide it. It's a good way to lose it, too!

The Spoils of War

People have been searching for the Hessian treasure ever since the days of America's War of Independence. It all began shortly after the defeat of General Burgoyne at Saratoga. Among the British general's troops were many hired Hessian soldiers who were more interested in looting and plundering the land than in fighting. Service in the army for many of them was merely an opportunity to ransack the towns they passed through. Over the months of fighting, they had accumulated quite a hoard of valuables.

After Burgoyne's defeat, many of these hired soldiers fled eastward in the general direction of Boston, carrying their stolen treasure with them.

News of their flight raced on ahead of them, and in Massachusetts a band of angry colonials was hastily organized to try and stop them before they could reach Boston. The group grew from a small band of farmers into a pursuing force that was large enough to stand against the veteran Hessians. The spot picked for the battle was near Dalton, in western Massachusetts.

The Hessians had several small cannons with them and some small arms. As they were shot at more and more from the hills, they decided to take a stand and fight it out with the farmer-soldiers who were attacking from all sides.

It soon became clear, however, that the Hessians had met their match and were fighting a losing battle. What could they do with their plundered loot? The only answer was to bury it, they decided, in hopes that someday, when the war was over, they could come back and dig it up.

Under cover of darkness, according to one story, the Hessians stuffed the money and jewels into the cannon barrels and buried them on the spot. Then, the angry colonials closed in.

After the battle was over, the few Hessians who remained alive did not know where the booty had been buried. That was almost two centuries ago, and since then many hundreds of folks have tried to find it. Perhaps some unsuspecting hunter has eaten his lunch right over the spot where the rusted cannons still guard the stolen treasure.

Great Lakes Gold

Lost or buried treasure generally brings forth a picture of palm trees, white sands and tropical waters. But exotic islands are not the only sites of long-lost treasure. In the Great Lakes alone, hundreds of ships have gone down with valuable cargoes. Along the shores of the inland lakes, too, treasure and gold have been buried for one reason or another and never found again.

Near Bayfield, Wisconsin, just to the east of a point of land running out into the western tip of Lake Superior, are the Apostle Islands. One of the smaller ones is called Hermit Island, and in the early days of the United States much fighting took place there between British and American troops. There were also small but bitter skirmishes between the British and hostile Indians.

A small British outpost on Hermit Island was the target of a good-size Indian force. The soldiers were particularly concerned, for they were guarding the payroll for many of the British troops in that part of the country. Exactly how much gold and silver made up this payroll is not known, but it had to be a considerable amount.

When the Indian attack seemed imminent, the officers decided to bury the money for safekeeping. A small group of trusted officers took the treasure to a remote part of the little island and buried it well. After covering up all signs of the digging, they returned to the main force to await the attack.

A bloody battle ensued, and all but two of the British soldiers were massacred on the spot. The two enlisted men who survived were badly wounded, but they managed to reach the mainland with news of the slaughter. The men knew about the buried payroll, but they had no idea where on the island it was hidden. To this day the treasure has not been found.

Somewhere on this little island in Lake Superior a hoard of old coins may still rest below the soil, guarded by roots and rocks that have shifted over it through the years. It may also be guarded by the ghosts of those who thought they were hiding it for a few days instead of forever.

In the Gardens of "Versailles"

The southern United States, for one reason or another, has long been said to contain many buried treasures. Legends even pinpoint these riches, as if all you'd need to find them were the will and a shovel. Somehow, though, they have eluded all seekers. Take, for example, some of the lost treasures of the Civil War plantations.

Many antebellum plantation owners kept their wealth in their mansions, either hidden in secret closets or behind walls or buried in the cellars in stone vaults. When the war broke out and the Union Army began to burn these houses, many Southerners hurriedly buried their gold and silver about their grounds. For various reasons, much of this bullion was never dug up again.

One such lost treasure belonged to Valcour Aime, said at one time to be the richest man in the South. Aime had built a magnificent palace, which became known as the "Little Versailles of Louisiana." He lived in it with his five daughters.

Each daughter married, with one exception—Aime's favorite, Gabrielle. Gabrielle was sent to France to learn the social graces. When she returned, many parties were given in her honor, and the aging Aime was delighted with her. She was apparently lovely and talented, and had learned her lessons well.

Just a few days after her return, however, Gabrielle became ill and shortly died of a fever. Rumors spread that she had caught the fever on the ship coming back from Paris, or even while in France. There were dark suspicions that it was not a fever at all but a disease that could not be mentioned.

Aime was heartbroken. His grief was increased by the death of his other daughters, one by one, until he was left alone with his fortune and a few slaves. His happy life had crumbled about his head. He no longer took an interest in the gardens, and the great house fell into ruins. Finally, when the Civil War broke out, he let all his slaves go, with the exception of one old black house servant who had been with him for 40 years.

The two old men stayed at the mansion until they were warned that the Yankees were approaching. Then Aime and his one remaining slave loaded his fortune into an old cart and hauled it out into the neglected gardens to hide it from the enemy.

By morning the deed was done. The treasure was

buried deep in the great gardens, but exactly where, no one has ever been able to determine. Both Aime and the old slave died before the war ended. To this day, millions in gold lie buried, perhaps, somewhere under "Little Versailles"—the huge palace that was practically a city. But where?

No Intention of Dying

Here is another tale of a lost Civil War plantation treasure, but it has its own curious twist. An enormously
wealthy gentleman named Hippolyte Chretien II lived
in a vast and magnificent plantation home in the Bayou
Teche country to the west of New Orleans. The family's
wealth went back to the days of the Spanish conquerors,
and both Jean and Pierre Lafitte often stopped off at the
plantation, possibly to leave their pirated loot in the
Chretiens' safekeeping.

Hippolyte II lived before the Civil War began, so his
treasure was not threatened by raiding Union armies.
Nevertheless, he was eccentric enough to believe that all
his millions had to be buried in the ground if he was to
have peace of mind. So he and a trusted slave named
Pajo secretly buried 37 boxes of gold beneath the trees of
his far-flung gardens. His wife, Félicité, begged him not
to do it, for should he die she would have no idea of where

to find the money to support herself. Hippolyte II, who was 71, replied that he had no intention of dying for a long while yet.

Strangely enough, shortly after he buried the gold, he came down with a fever and almost at once slipped off into a coma. He was thus unable to tell his wife where she could find the gold. Félicité was panic-stricken. She had great grief for her dying husband and considerable doubt about finding the family fortune. Hippolyte II slipped deeper into his coma and died within three hours. After the funeral Félicité called old Pajo to her chambers and asked if he knew where his master had hidden the fortune. All Pajo said was that they had buried it at night under a tree some distance from the house, and that he just wasn't sure which tree it was.

Félicité with Pajo then hunted through all the yards and gardens, but could find no trace of either digging or of any depression where a hole might have been. Perhaps, for further secrecy, Hippolyte II had changed the location and moved the gold bit by bit so that only he knew where it was buried. Certainly Pajo couldn't or wouldn't share the secret.

The search continued through two more generations. Finally, the plantation was impoverished. The house passed into the grasping hands of a moneylender. Still the fortune eludes all who seek it. Perhaps Hippolyte II disproved the saying "You can't take it with you," and in some mysterious manner *did.*

5. LEGENDS OF TREASURE

- "Money lights" hover over buried treasure in South America.

- An old Indian woman hunts for her share of the gold from a wagon train massacre.

- A lonely prospector's "lucky" pick becomes lucky indeed for a little Mexican boy.

- A cave you could see only when the August moon was full—plus a nine-foot-tall Indian ghost—was Henry telling the truth?

- Where do elephants go to die?

The "Money Lights" of South America

Perhaps you've seen the soft, mysterious glow of phosphorus in an old rotting stump while you were off camping at night, or flashing lights on the surface of a tropical ocean. These are natural phenomena, but you've probably never seen the unexplainable "money lights" of Mexico and Peru.

These so-called "luces del dinero" are well known to the natives. They claim that wherever you see these mysterious lights hovering over the rocky soil or along a jungle trail, there you'll find treasure. They say that the long gold trail from Potosé, Bolivia, to Tucumán, Argentina, where the Spanish used to travel, is pitted with holes where generations of treasure-hunters have dug when these eerie lights winked at them.

According to the natives, if you see one of these tall wavering lights, you should drive a stake quickly into the ground where it glowed and then go away until daylight. Never try to dig when the light is there, for where there is the light there are also demons—"demonios"—who attack the careless treasure-seeker.

Legend has it that some of these "money lights" move along the ground like green pythons, while others stand upright. Some are white, some of a pale greenish color, and some burn with a blue flame. No scientific explanation has ever been found for them.

One man reported that he dug where he saw one such "luz del dinero" to prove that it was all a myth and a mere superstition. Now he's not so sure, for just under the surface of the ground he found a rich gold deposit, now a real mine. A mining engineer said that he almost always found metal ore beneath where the "money lights" flickered.

Another skeptic rented an old Mexican hacienda because an old woman told him that she had often seen the "money light" around the house. The tenant searched the floors and walls and courtyard but found nothing. But who can say that the old lady had not been right after all? The next tenant also looked for the treasure—and found it. Under the rafters, well hidden in the roof, he found a metal container full of gold doubloons, a small fortune. After that, the light was seen no more.

They say that the "money lights" that burn with a blue

flame sometimes cover the entire area of the treasure buried beneath it. The "flames" never burn the grass or vegetation around them, although some are reported to flicker and dart like true flames.

Dead Men Do Tell Tales

A legend of dead men who *did* tell tales, even if they were to no avail, is set in Oklahoma, near the Wichita Mountains, at a time when homesteaders were beginning to till the soil and establish their farms.

It started when some of the townsfolk began to find things not usually found just below the sod. In a valley called Devil's Canyon, bones and human skulls were dug up. Rumors circulated. Could Devil's Canyon have been an Indian cemetery, an old tribal battleground, the scene of a massacre? No one knew. In time, interest slackened. Occasionally a bit of metal, a ring of steel, a few nails, or other rusty trinkets appeared, but they were casually tossed aside in the more serious business of getting farms started and crops ready for winter.

Several years later an old Indian woman appeared in the valley and began to poke about. She would mutter to herself as she moved here and there among the rocks and dry ravines in the vicinity of where the bones had been plowed up. She was ignored by all until a few chance remarks revealed that she was looking for a long-buried treasure.

Questioning her produced only stony silence and suspicious looks. She continued to poke about the hills, often sitting on a rock and staring here and there as if in deep thought. A harmless old crone, most homesteaders thought, but a few had other ideas and set to work to find out more about this "treasure."

With the aid of a potent liquid offered in a spirit of sudden "friendliness," the aged squaw divulged that she was the sole survivor of an Indian band that had massacred a wagon train on that very spot many years ago. Her part of the share, to be divided with her brave, had been two wagonloads of gold ore and nuggets. At that time the Indians had no way to work the ore and dared not try to spend the nuggets. They had buried the treasure nearby at the foot of Twin Mountain, to the west of the place where the bones of the massacred wagon-train members had been plowed up. Other Indians had also buried their shares nearby, but she had no idea just where.

For weeks the homesteaders, along with the old woman, tried to locate the buried ore, to no avail. One night she wandered off and was never seen again. The treasure of the Devil's Canyon has never been found, even though the dead men of the furrows told a part of the tale of massacre, plunder, and buried gold so near and yet so very far away.

The "Lucky" Pick

This story, as the writer heard it, took place in Mexico, somewhere in the section known as Coahuilla, up near the little settlement of La Babia.

It seems there was an old prospector roaming the hills looking for gold. He always carried a rusty old pick. When asked why he didn't get a newer pick or a better one or clean up this ancient tool, he would mutter something about its being a "lucky" pick that would help him find his fortune.

Finally, around the turn of the century, the prospector did make a small strike. He immediately began digging a tunnel in the side of a river. For days he dug, carrying the dirt down to the river and dumping it, so that the current would carry it off and help conceal the size of the huge hole he was creating. He was afraid that if others saw the size of the tunnel they would suspect that he had found an immense fortune and perhaps kill him. Actually he had not much money, but, as he dug further, he did manage to keep himself going, even though on short rations.

The only friend the prospector had was a little Mexican boy who came by almost every day to watch him dig. The boy brought him fresh water from the river and occasionally a little food from his home. He also kept watch for strangers who might spy upon the old prospector while he worked.

One day the little boy, sitting by the tunnel entrance with his dog, saw a rifleman approaching from the river bank on horseback. He called inside to warn the old miner. The old man hurried out to the entrance, driving his lucky pick into one of the tunnel walls inside. As the miner came out of the tunnel, the man on the horse fired his rifle and shot the old man fatally. Before the prospector died, however, he told the young boy that he was leaving the mine to him and that he hoped his pick would bring the child the luck it had never quite brought to him. The rifleman, seeing that the old man was dead and that the boy had witnessed the slaying, rode off, concealing his face with his hands. He was never found.

The boy hung the old miner's hat on the pick stuck into the wall, and went for help, but it was too late. He told the adults what the old man had said about the mine, and they all laughingly agreed that it was his—for what it was worth.

Later they were to envy him his good fortune. Sometime later, the young lad went to the mine, determined to keep on with the digging. When he pulled the old pick from the tunnel wall a big section of the rock broke loose, revealing a vein of almost pure gold that had been only a few inches beyond where the old man had dug. It was indeed a "lucky pick" for the little boy who had be-friended the lonely old prospector.

The Cave of the August Moon

Mt. Van Hoevenberg, New York, was named after the Dutch Henry Van Hoevenberg, a famous innkeeper and explorer. Many fabulous tales were told about him. Some of them could have happened, though it's hard to believe that the following one ever did.

As the story goes, Henry was hiking in his beloved woods when he came across an old parchment map inscribed with the characters of the Algonquin language. Actually, the Algonquins are not known to have *had* a written language. But, nevertheless, Harry said that the map gave directions to a vast buried treasure.

The treasure was supposed to be hidden in a cave partway up Mt. Colden, but the cave entrance could only be seen from another mountain, Mt. McIntyre, when the August moon was at its fullest. This information frustrated Henry because it was then September and he had to wait a whole year to investigate further. But wait he did. The night of the full moon the following August found him over 5,000 feet up the rugged slope of McIntyre scanning Colden for any signs of a cave entrance. And there it was, a dark opening just above a precipice.

Henry, so the story goes, scrambled down McIntyre and up Colden. He found the cave, paused to catch his breath, and then, lighting a small birch-bark torch, entered, peering ahead of him into the vault.

Back several yards from the entrance, he spotted several old leather trunks, their handles and sides split and cracked with age. From the broken sides a trickle of gold coins had already fallen to the cave's rock floor. He had begun to fill his pockets with the coins when he heard a sound behind him, coming from still further back in the cave. Suddenly a transparent nine-foot-tall Indian was bearing down on him with a scalping knife raised above his feathered head. Henry dropped the coins to seize the torch, but before he could get it, the Indian giant was upon him and the fight began. The torch was stomped out as they struggled furiously in the dark.

Although Henry was short, he was strong, and he fought fiercely. Soon, however, he was shoved over the edge of the cliff into the void below. He remembered his fall being broken by a small tree and then he remembered crashing onto the ground far below. Later he crawled to the shore of Heart Lake, where he was found by searchers. He had two broken legs, three broken ribs, and a broken arm, but also, we are told, gold and wampum in his pockets to prove his story.

Disbelievers taunted Henry and tried to goad him into returning to the cave. Henry stiffly refused. He maintained that he had found the Indian ghost far too unpleasant and unsociable.

Elephants' Graveyard

Africa, the so-called Dark Continent, is full of buried treasure of assorted types, and a thousand and one tales of intrigue.

In spite of all that is done intentionally and otherwise to dispel these tales, many of them persist. Tales of buried treasure have been proven false time and again, yet adventurers brave privation and even death seeking the very diamonds they have been assured never existed in the first place. Many of these courageous souls believe that they are being told the treasure is not there just so that others can find it first.

One of the most persistent African rumors is the myth of the "elephants' graveyard," somewhere in the vast interior—that place where old and wounded elephants go to die, and where a vast collection of ivory awaits some bold adventurer.

Some say it is in Kenya, others that it is in Zaïre, and some swear they know just where it is in Uganda. Some even claim that it is in a place where there never has been an elephant, because the elephants only go there to die.

One enterprising fellow, a few years ago, contacted the Bell Helicopter Company in Buffalo, New York, with a weird scheme. He at first merely asked questions about the helicopters—how far they would fly, cost figures, and so forth. He was very vague about what the whirlybird was to be used for, but when a Bell salesman finally pinned him down, he revealed that he and some other men had a marvelous idea for making a fortune. They were going to take the aircraft to Africa, find an old bull elephant, wound him slightly—but enough so that he would think he was going to die—and then follow him with the helicopter until he led them to the elephants' graveyard and riches. The deal fell through.

Actually there is no such thing as a so-called "graveyard" for old and retiring elephants except in the minds of fortune hunters. Old elephants pass on to greener pastures like any other creature, just where they happen to be when their time is up. They do, however, usually leave the herd to die alone with the dignity that such great animals are entitled to in their final hour.

Eventually, other creatures of the area consume what is left and even the ivory tusks vanish beneath the drifting sands or lush vegetation, or sink into marshes or soft soil. African hunters occasionally come upon the last mortal remains of these great beasts, but usually nothing is left except a few traces that prove once there was a great animal.

6. TREASURE FOUND

- Treasure is sometimes found in very ordinary places.

- Were they birds' eggs, marbles or diamonds—the clay balls the young man threw in the sea?

- Do Blackbeard's millions lie beneath the sands at Plum Point?

- A dream reveals long-hidden treasure in Tucson.

Extraordinary Finds in Ordinary Places

Treasures have been found in unlikely places—not by wild-eyed adventurers, but by sober people doing everyday chores. Here's a sampling:

A farmer in Illinois struck his shovel against something hard while he was digging for fishworms. At first he thought it was a stone. When he saw it was an earthenware pot, he idly pried open the top and found it filled with almost $15,000 worth of gold coins.

Another Illinois farmer, near Freeport, found nearly $4,000 in two very rusty old baking-powder cans hidden in his barn. Neither farmer ever discovered where his unexpected wealth had come from.

A miner working a claim near Gold Beach, Oregon, was amazed when he unearthed several thousand dollars' worth of Spanish coins dated 1700 and 1734.

A Salisbury, Connecticut, man by the name of Vance Butler found nearly $30,000 in gold coins in an old graveyard near his home.

In the state of Michoacan, Mexico, two masons replastering an old stable wall found over $100,000 in Spanish gold hidden there by the rebel general José Davalos.

A Mexican farmer in the state of Oaxaca turned up nearly $250,000 in gold in one of his fields, said to have been buried by a bandit gang headed by the notorious El Solo. And so the record goes.

The Balls of Clay

While on vacation in Florida the young man spent a lot of time wandering along the sparsely populated coastline looking for interesting odds and ends—unusual shells, pieces of driftwood, and bits of wreckage from ships.

On one of these beachcombing trips he noticed a small hole partway up a low cliff. Curious, he climbed up and looked into the opening. Perhaps a pirate treasure, hidden chest or something equally exciting might be there.

He peered into the long tapering passage that ran a couple of feet back into the ledge, but he could see nothing in the gloom. Cautiously, he put his hand into the far corners to see if anything had been tucked in back. Sure enough, against the back wall of the opening, his hand touched what felt like birds' eggs or marbles—a little pile of them.

Gathering up a handful, he brought them into the light. They varied from about the size of a large pea to almost the size of a golf ball, and they all were round and smooth and apparently made of a hard grey clay. Certainly they had no value, he thought in disappointment, but he filled his pockets with about two dozen of the "marbles" and climbed down to the sandy shore below.

As he walked along the beach, he occasionally threw one of the clay balls at floating driftwood or skittered them out to see how many "skips" they would make over the surface of the ocean. Finally they were all gone.

A few days later the young man returned to his home in the Midwest. As he was unpacking his vacation clothes, he discovered one of the smallest of the clay balls, overlooked in the bottom of his pocket. He tossed it into a drawer as a souvenir of his "find" in the cliff cave.

Not long after, he and a friend who was interested in pirate lore were talking about some of the famous buccaneers who had hidden treasure along the Florida coasts. When his friend told him that some of the pirates used to hide precious stones in small clay balls, the young man described the balls in the little cave. They laughed over what he had done with the "precious stones"—and forgot the incident.

Afterwards, when he remembered the small pellet he had saved, the young man's curiosity was aroused. Quickly he began to scrape away the hardened clay from his souvenir. At first there was nothing but clay. Then the mass cracked—and out rolled a small but perfect blue-white diamond. What had been in the other clay balls that he had tossed into the sea?

Who Got What?

One of the most intriguing tales of a lucky treasure find comes from North Carolina. For more than 200 years tales of buried treasure have centered around a narrow strip of land called Plum Point, where Bath Creek flows into the Pamlico River.

The story goes that Blackbeard, the famous pirate, once came ashore on Plum Point, buried a good-sized chest, and sailed away, never to return. As a result, Plum Point is worked over year after year by would-be treasure finders. So far, though, only one incident has even hinted that part of Blackbeard's millions may have been there. Since a partial find could suggest that more remains, this strange account has intrigued treasure-trovers ever since.

It happened in 1928. Two men, deciding to try their luck on the point, gathered up tools, plus optimism and enthusiasm, and started out. When they got to the point they tried to figure out where, and just how, they would have buried a treasure had they been Blackbeard. Finally they struck off across the dunes. They may have picked the right spot, but if so, they were too late.

Almost to the dune where they had decided that there might be treasure (so the report goes), they stumbled across a pit in the sand, partially lined with very old bricks. About the crumbling brick walls were piles of freshly dug dirt. Many more old bricks were scattered about in tossed confusion, and there was a rough tripod made of heavy timbers, such as one would use to raise a heavy load from below ground.

The partners stared at each other in mingled astonishment and frustration, then jumped into the pit and examined the "floor" of the ancient vault. There, in the packed sand, was the unmistakable imprint of the bottom of a barred and riveted chest of good size. The chest was gone and so were all traces of the lucky finders. Some versions of the report say that all that was left was a grinning skull propped up on the pile of sand overlooking the opened pit.

To this day no one knows who found the treasure and what, if anything, that treasure was. But many Plum Pointers believe there's more for the digging.

A Dream of Treasure

Harry Behn, of Greenwich, Connecticut, noted Indian authority and author, has gold-mined and generally hunted treasure and excitement in both near and remote places. This incident took place in Tucson, Arizona.

Near where Behn and his wife were staying, a Mexican lived alone in a small adobe and stucco house, an unassuming place with a well and some trees around it. The Behns paid little attention to either the house or its inhabitant.

However, after they returned from a month's field trip, they were astonished to find that the house had become a shambles. The walls were hacked, the roof was partially gone and holes had been dug in the small yard, leaving piles of earth and rubble. The Mexican was gone.

Behn was curious and asked questions around town. The answers were startling. It seems that the Mexican had suddenly appeared at the local bank with handfuls of Old Spanish coins, pieces of eight, doubloons, and other ancient coins of considerable value.

The bank had redeemed them, and then the man told his astonishing story. He had dreamed one night that the well in the yard of the house on Old Wetmore Road (now known as Timberlost Drive) contained a long-hidden treasure. Not really believing that his dreams would come true, the next morning he began to poke deep in the well's gloomy interior.

At the bottom his fingers encountered something hard and slimy. Perhaps a broken pot or an old kettle accidentally dropped in the well, he thought. Poking further, he brought up several black, round and thin objects that just might be coins, long buried under water and mud. Hurriedly, he cleaned them off. They *were* coins, and the old kettle was full of them.

After redeeming the coins at the bank and telling his story, which immediately flew around Tucson, the Mexican went to Mexico to visit his family.

That accounted for some of the damage to the house! But not all. While the now wealthy owner was in Mexico, Tucson people drove to his house and took it apart, looking for more treasure. Each night the house was battered by heavy axes in eager hands. By the time the Mexican returned, the place was beyond repair. He left for Greenwich Village, New York, never to return.

7. THE MOST FRUSTRATING TREASURES

- How close have you come to buried treasure? Perhaps closer than you know.

- Silver bars lie on a reef in the Atlantic—off the Florida Keys.

- No one can find and hold onto the booty of bad Dan Dunham.

- An iron chest evades capture in a crystal-clear spring.

Picnic Treasure Hunt

You'll never know how close you may have been to buried treasure. Imagine how upsetting it would be to learn that if you had dug a hole six inches deeper, you would have come up with Blackbeard's millions!

A misfortune like this once befell Harry Behn, an author mentioned in the last chapter. When working in the Southwest, he read a book called *Coronado's Children*. In it were several accounts of Spanish and Mexican buried treasure, and one location was close to where he was living.

Behn decided to search it out. To make the treasure hunt more fun, he took along his wife and two of their friends. The group found a site that looked right and got to work with shovels, muscles, and enthusiasm, joking about getting rich before lunch.

Nothing turned up, however, and they finally decided to eat beside a little brook running past their digging operations and dug into the sandwiches.

Several years later Behn read a newspaper story about how another reader of *Coronado's Children* had also decided to look for the treasure *and had found it*. While Behn had been playing at his "expedition," the treasure—two old Spanish cannon, their bores filled with pure melted silver—had been right beside him, lying among the pebbles in the bottom of the cool brook, a few feet from where he had eaten lunch.

The Reef at Key West

In 1935 a veteran fisherman named Charlie sailed from his home port of Miami to Key West. He had planned a short trip, but a violent storm kept him at the Key.

After the storm passed, he set out for home in his sloop. The weather was fine, the breeze steady and the sun bright. Charlie dozed at the helm as his little craft plowed through the waves, picking its own course.

Suddenly the boat ran onto a reef a couple of feet below the surface and heeled over, awakening Charlie with a start. The sloop came to a standstill, balanced at a slight angle on the coral below. Charlie slipped over the side into the waist-deep water to inspect the hull for damage and shove the craft off again into deep water.

As he worked his way around the grounded craft, he noticed that the small reef was covered with bars or small blocks of dark metal. He ducked down and lifted one to the surface. It was heavy and black and looked like pig iron or lead. The top of the reef for several hundred feet was littered with these bars.

Apparently, a ship carrying pig iron or lead bars had been wrecked on the reef and these were all that were left. He hefted the bar in his hand. It weighed about 60 pounds and would make good ballast, so he loaded sixteen of them aboard his sloop. In a short time he worked his boat loose and continued on to Miami.

He thought nothing more of the metal bars until about two years later, when his boat was pulled up for an overhaul at a local shipyard. He unloaded the bars, piled them on the dock, and sat next to them while he ate lunch. Absentmindedly, he began to pick at the dark crust on one of the bars. Inside, he found a shiny metal that looked like lead. Out of curiosity, he took it to a jeweler friend for testing. The bars were not lead at all, but pure silver. He had been sailing around with a small fortune in his ship's bilge for two years!

Ever since then, he and others have vainly sought the silver-plated reef somewhere off the Florida Keys. Apparently, the storm had uncovered the bars on the shallow reef, but since then another storm had covered them again. Somewhere they still await a lucky sailor who may get to the reef at just the right moment—between storms.

The Vanishing Mule Pen

The "mule pen treasure" has produced more frustration than any other lost hoard, because two people have been right on top of it without knowing what was at their feet.

A famous Western badman named Dan Dunham returned from Mexico in 1860, after several months of looting and robbery. With him were a group of his followers and 31 mules loaded with all the loot they had gathered while below the border. As the desperadoes worked their way along the Nueces River six or seven miles below the Laredo Crossing, following a trail on the south side of the river, they were attacked by a band of Indians.

They seemed to be fighting the attackers off successfully, but it looked as if it would be a long battle. Under cover of darkness the outlaws hurriedly threw up a couple of fieldstone stockades for better protection. One pen was for the mules and the other for the men.

They herded the mules into the stone pen, unloaded their treasure from the animals' backs and buried it in the ground. Then the mules were turned loose to trample the dirt and remove all signs of digging inside the stone walls. The fight continued for several days. The situation finally became desperate. Dunham decided to go to a fort some miles away for help. Although seriously injured, he finally arrived, but in such bad shape that he gave incoherent directions about where the pens and the rest of his group were.

Weeks later, when he was well again, he tried to retrace his steps. But he never could find the pens. Eventually he died at the fort. No one has ever found the treasure.

Yet at least two people have been right there, unaware of the significance of the stone pens. In 1866, a cowboy named Pete McNeill spent a stormy night in one of them and wondered what such pens were doing out in that wild country. Later, after hearing the story, he tried to find them again—but his search was in vain.

More recently a judge from San Antonio camped near the pens while he was on a hunting trip. Since he had never heard the story either, he did not make a note of their location. Afterwards, he too tried to find them and the treasure they held—without success. Others have told similar stories about being on the spot, but no one has ever managed a second visit.

The Elusive Chest

No known hidden treasure has frustrated more trovers than the one in the crystal-clear waters of Ponce de Leon Spring, about seven miles north of Deland, Florida. A group of Spaniards was once attacked by Seminole Indians there. When they saw that defeat and probable annihilation would be their fate, they heaved a heavy iron money chest into the spring so that their attackers would not get it.

One of the Spaniards escaped and struggled back to Tampa, where he reported the attack and the sinking of the chest, but as the Seminoles were still on the rampage, no one dared go back to recover it.

In the 1920s two boys swimming underwater spotted the iron chest resting on a narrow ledge on the rocky side of the spring. Excited, they hurried home for ropes with which to haul it to the surface, but when they returned the chest had slipped from the shelf of rock and vanished into the depths below.

In 1939 two divers descended through the clear water to the bottom, where they found the chest and attached a rope to one of its two handles. As they were hauling it up the rope broke and the chest sank, not merely to the bottom but *through* it—into a turbulent opening through which the water rose to fill the pool.

The spring pool is about 100 feet in diameter and 40 feet deep. The bottom is of quicksand consistency, and the opening is a six-foot hole. Occasionally, the iron chest rises briefly, driven up by the powerful current, and it has been seen by a number of people visiting the pool.

After each brief trip up into the pool, the chest apparently sinks back down through the opening to whatever is below, until a combination of effects heaves it up again to astonish and frustrate those who spot it.

This elusive treasure chest cannot help but stimulate speculation as to how to capture it. Would it be possible for a man with a steel mesh "landing net" to scoop it out as it boiled up from the depths? Could he at least secure it temporarily, so that it could be cabled to the shore and hauled up later with a winch?

Could an expert skindiver with an aqua lung swim down through that six-foot opening, attach a steel cable to one of the chest's handles, and return alive?

Certainly many methods have been tried, and none has succeeded so far.

The Ruby Cat

A famous jewel thief, who was known by the name of Klaus Gudden, arrived in Germany in 1894. He had with him two fabulous matched rubies. The jewels had originally been the eyes of a statue in a Korean temple. That was in about 165 A.D. Then they were stolen from the statue. In 1560 they were acquired by the sultan of the Ottoman Empire. He in turn gave them to a lady. The rubies cost her her life, when a thief killed her to get them. Later they belonged to Louis XV, who gave them to Madame Pompadour. She eventually sold them to a Russian nobleman. How Klaus Gudden got them will probably never be known.

In any event, as soon as he appeared in Berlin, the police began searching for him. He was caught and, as he tried to escape, he was shot and killed. But the jewels were not found. A few years later, a gem expert named Graves tried to find out what happened to them. Rubies like that couldn't vanish into thin air, he reasoned. Undoubtedly, Gudden had hidden them in hopes that he could return for them later.

Mr. Graves learned that when the police set their dragnet, Gudden was trapped in a certain block in Berlin. He had been unable to leave that block for several days. Searching for clues in that limited area, Graves discovered that Gudden had visited a little ceramic shop on the very day that he had been killed. The shop specialized in clay cats.

Then Graves learned that Gudden had picked up one cat that had just been removed from the kiln and looked it over for several minutes. He asked the owner to set it aside for him until he returned. He scratched an "X" on the bottom, and made the owner promise that that particular cat would not be sold to anyone else.

When the shop owner learned that his strange customer had been killed, he sent the cat out in a shipment with dozens of others just like it.

Graves traced the shipment to America, but there the trail branched out in a hundred directions. The cats had been sold all over the country and it was impossible to trace them all.

One of those cats may hold within its clay body a half-million dollars in rubies. Eight inches high, it lies in a reclining position with its tail wrapped around its body and forepaws. It was originally yellow, but by now it must be darker, cracked and chipped with age. The faint "X" on the bottom may no longer be visible. But the years will not have damaged the fortune it guards.

Marie Antoinette's Necklace

Among the many famous tales of vanished treasure that fill the pages of history, one of the most baffling is the legend of Marie Antoinette's fabulous diamond necklace.

Just before the French Revolution, two jewelers in league with two cardinals forced Marie Antoinette to purchase a magnificent necklace. Its price was six million pounds (about twelve million dollars).

During the hectic days of the Revolution, the cardinals feared for the necklace's safety and secretly sent it to England. From there it was sent to Canada, the haven of many exiled Frenchmen. Its fate after that was never known.

Towards the end of the 18th century a Frenchman, accompanied by an Indian, came from Canada to a small town near what is now Nashua, New Hampshire. The two lived in a little hut on a wooded road leading to Pennichuck Pond. All the years he lived there, the Frenchman gave the impression that he had some great secret, but no one knew what it was. From time to time the Indian went back to Canada, and then returned months later. While the Indian was away, the Frenchman left his hut only for food or other vital supplies. Occasionally, he walked along the edge of the little pond, apparently deep in thought.

During one of the Indian's trips, the Frenchman died. When the Indian got back, he was greatly upset over the death of his companion, and left again after a few days.

Some years later, he came back again. Carefully, trying not to arouse suspicion, he began to ask guarded questions about a beautiful string of wampum. It had been in the care of the Frenchman, he said, in trust for officials in Canada. When the two first arrived, they had buried it somewhere along the shore of Pennichuck Pond. Now he couldn't find it.

No one knew anything about the string of wampum. But the local people had heard of the famous diamond necklace, brought years ago from a far-off land. Had that been what the Frenchman was guarding?

A long and excited search began, but to this day no one knows if somewhere along the shores of tiny Pennichuck Pond a "string of wampum"—the fabulous necklace of Marie Antoinette—still lies buried beneath the soil.

8. WILD WILD WEST

- There are things in the Big Horn Mountains of greater value than gold.

- Indian attacks defeat two attempts to get at the riches in Crazy Woman Creek. Is the treasure still there?

- Old fires and burned wagons on the Great Plains were often signs of buried treasure. That might be worth remembering.

Lost Big Horn Gold

No one knows how much treasure may have been kept secret by those who had good reason to hush it up. This is certainly the case with the gold in the Big Horn Mountains of Wyoming.

Father Jeanne-Pierre de Smet, the famed Jesuit missionary who clambered in and out of the Rockies for nearly a quarter-century, was a friend to several Native American tribes. He knew gold when he saw it, and he saw much of it, with the aid of friendly Indians.

Presumably in gratitude for the priest's spiritual guidance, certain tribes showed him huge gold deposits in the Big Horn Mountains. The Jesuit records that he was "astonished at their size and richness," but warned the Indians to continue to keep their gold secret. He had ample reason for suspecting that droves of white prospectors would overrun the country, seize the gold, and drive the natives from their hunting lands. He not only urged them never to reveal the locations of the lodes but promised to keep his own mouth shut.

The Indians agreed, and Father de Smet took his secret to the grave. But traders and scholars who know where he travelled believe that gold in the millions must still be hidden somewhere in the towering mountains of Wyoming.

Another find was hushed up in the mid-1800s, according to the famous western guide, mountaineer, and trader, Jim Bridger. Bridger, too, knew gold when he saw it.

In the summer of 1859, Bridger was leading the Reynolds expedition across northern Wyoming when he stopped for a drink at a shallow mountain stream. As he bent over, his eye caught a golden flash on the bottom. He plunged his hands into the water and brought up two palmsful of pure golden nuggets. He quietly called Captain Reynolds to his side and showed him the find. Reynolds was at once concerned that should his men learn of it they might then and there give up exploring for gold-hunting, and his army career would come to an abrupt end.

He ordered Bridger to throw the nuggets away and keep their location secret. Jim did as ordered. He didn't even mention the find until years later, and never specified its location. If Bridger's silence smacks of the weird, so does Captain Reynolds'. He never revealed the secret either, not even after he'd retired from the army.

So somewhere in the Big Horn Mountains of Wyoming a small mountain stream may still flow over a fortune in gold, waiting perhaps for less dedicated people to find it.

Somewhere Near Crazy Woman Creek

One of the most interesting lost-mine stories to come out of the Rocky Mountain region is that of the famous Lost Cabin Mine somewhere along Crazy Woman Creek in the Big Horn Mountains of Wyoming. There are several versions of the story, but all are basically the same. It goes like this.

Three men are said to have found this fabulously rich mine. One was Allen Hulbert from Wisconsin, and the two others were named Cox and Jones. Venturing into unknown and unexplored Yellowstone territory, then full of hostile Indians, they came upon traces of gold in one of the upper branches of Crazy Woman Creek and patiently followed them upstream towards the anticipated mother lode. Finally, after days of patient panning and searching, they found the vein and began to sink a shaft deep into the rock to get out the rich ore.

As winter came on, they stopped work long enough to build a crude log cabin and erect a log stockade around it for protection against a surprise attack. As yet they had seen no signs of Indians. When spring came they went back to work and brought out more gold to add to their store of treasure.

One day, as the three men were approaching their mine, Hulbert remembered something he had left at the cabin and went back to get it. He was hardly out of sight of his partners when he heard two gun shots. He quietly retraced his steps and was horrified to see Indians clustered about his partners' bodies. He raced back to the cabin and after hurriedly burying most of the gold they had collected, he took what was left and set out southeast to get help.

Nearly three weeks later he met a wagon train full of gold seekers. He showed them the pieces of gold he had, told them about his strike and offered to take them to it if they would protect him from the Indians. He planned to take the gold he had buried for himself and leave the mine to them.

They agreed. But after many weeks of searching, Hulbert was forced to admit that he was lost. He could not find the cabin or the mine. The enraged gold hunters nearly killed him, but he finally got away and was last seen in Virginia City, Montana, in 1864, a broken, poverty-stricken man.

It is said that later on others found the cabin and mine, worked it for a while and also were attacked by Indians, with a single man escaping. He too proved the mine was there by showing nuggets and an arrow wound received in the attack, but like Hulbert, he too was unable to retrace his steps to the "Lost Cabin Mine." Somewhere along the upper reaches of Crazy Woman Creek there may still remain a fabulously rich gold strike for some lucky prospectors to find for the third time.

They can search with one comforting thought—Indians are no longer on the warpath in Wyoming.

Fortune Fires

The trails of the pioneers across the great Western plains are peppered with the charred remains of burned wagons. Some are covered with drifting sand and then uncovered again by the winds. They are hard to conceal permanently for there are many metal parts that last for years, even after fire has reduced them mostly to ashes. Some of these burned wagons cover fortunes in buried treasure.

Often a wagon train was overtaken by Indians and burned. A single wagon or two might escape, but could not go on alone. It was the custom of their owners to bury in the ground any gold they could not carry with them and burn their wagon over the spot. The wagon served as a blackened marker for the gold's future recovery, as well as camouflage, since the rest of the train lay charred around it. The remains of an evening campfire served a similar purpose, but only for short-term departures from the loot. The burned-wagon marker served for such treasure as had to be left behind for a long time.

For example, in 1850 a party of pioneers stole corn from Indians in Nevada, and later the Indians destroyed their train, killing many people. One man killed was a jeweller travelling West to set up his business. He had with him many fine watches, gold, and gems. After the raid the jeweller and his loot were buried in side-by-side holes. Wagons destroyed in the raid were heaped over the spot and burned as markers.

A relative of the jeweller later tried to find the spot, but winds had covered it completely. Some time after that, the wagon marker was found by a man who had not heard of the treasure underneath. When he learned the facts and went back, the traces had once more been covered with drifting sands. The treasure may still be there.

*   *   *

Another authenticated report of a "fortune fire" reveals that in 1853 a small, wealthy party camped for the night far from the regular trail through the Colorado desert. They hid all their gold under the campfire and retired to their wagon, as advised by veteran travellers. During the night they were attacked by Indians. Their wagon was set afire by flaming arrows, and they were all slain as they emerged, one by one. No one has ever found the ruins of this burned wagon and its nearby buried treasure.

*   *   *

Another party buried a fortune in gold dust near Signal Hill in San Diego County, California. They were returning from a successful trip to the gold fields and had buried their booty under their campfire. They too were all killed in the night, and their treasure remains under the ashes.

*   *   *

Not all old fires or burned wagons conceal buried treasure, but it might be worthwhile to do a bit of digging underneath any one found in the far West. . . .

Index

About the Author

Given the name Carroll Burleigh Colby when he was born in Claremont, New Hampshire, in 1904, it didn't take long for C.B. Colby to rebel and begin using the initials "C.B." It was as C.B. Colby that he launched his career as author and illustrator, a career that spanned over 50 years and during which he published over 100 books, written mostly for young readers. Through the years, he also acted as editor of *Air Trails* and *Air Progress* magazines, aviation editor of *Popular Science Monthly*, and camping editor of *Outdoor Life* magazine. He was one of the founders of the Aviation Space Writers Association, and served on the Board of Directors of the Outdoor Writers Association. The pieces in this book were originally prepared for a column that appeared in the *White Plains Reporter Dispatch*. "I have always tried to make my latest book the BEST," he wrote, "to see the subjects through the inquisitive eyes of myself when I was a boy and to tell about them as I would have liked to have read about them."